The *STEM* of

Robots

By Derek Miller

Cavendish
Square

New York

Library of Congress Cataloging-in-Publication Data

Names: Miller, Derek L., author.
Title: The STEM of robots / Derek Miller.
Description: First edition. | New York : Cavendish Square, 2021. | Series: The world of STEM | Includes bibliographical references and index.
Identifiers: LCCN 2019042223 (print) | LCCN 2019042224 (ebook) | ISBN 9781502650269 (library binding) | ISBN 9781502650245 (paperback) | ISBN 9781502650252 (set) | ISBN 9781502650276 (ebook)
Subjects: LCSH: Robots–Juvenile literature. | Automation–Juvenile literature.
Classification: LCC TJ211.2 .M545 2021 (print) | LCC TJ211.2 (ebook) | DDC 629.8/92–dc23
LC record available at https://lccn.loc.gov/2019042223
LC ebook record available at https://lccn.loc.gov/2019042224

Editor: Caitlyn Miller and Jennifer Lombardo
Copy Editor: Alex Tessman
Designer: Andrea Davison-Bartolotta

The photographs in this book are used by permission and through the courtesy of: Cover, p. 1 Phonlamai Photo/Shutterstock.com; series art (background texture) bestbrk/Shutterstock.com; p. 4 JCDH/Shutterstock.com; p. 6 Poul Riishede/Shutterstock.com; p. 7 Sasin Tipchai/Shutterstock.com; p. 8 courtesy of NASA; p. 10 Jenson/Shutterstock.com; pp. 12–13 Matee Nuserm/Shutterstock.com; p. 14 Cathy Crawford/Photolibrary/Getty Images Plus; p. 15 Badias/Andia/Universal Images Group via Getty Images; pp. 16–17 science photo/Shutterstock.com; p. 18 adriaticfoto/Shutterstock.com; p. 20 Ben Birchall/PA Images via Getty Images; p. 22 marekuliasz/Shutterstock.com; p. 23 Erik Simonsen/Photographer's Choice/Getty Images Plus; p. 24 Oliver Burston/Ikon Images/Getty Images Plus; p. 26 Smith Collection/Gado/Getty Images; p. 28 ROBYN BECK/AFP via Getty Images; p. 29 (left) Zhang Yin/China News Service/Visual China Group via Getty Images; p. 29 (right) TOSHIFUMI KITAMURA/AFP via Getty Images.

Some of the images in this book illustrate individuals who are models. The depictions do not imply actual situations or events.

CPSIA compliance information: Batch #CS20CSQ: For further information contact Cavendish Square Publishing LLC, New York, New York, at 1-877-980-4450.

Printed in the United States of America

Find us on

Contents

ROBOTS ALL AROUND

Robots are machines that do things on their own. They don't need a human to help them do tasks that humans often do themselves. Some robots are ordinary. Pool-cleaning robots vacuum the bottom of most pools. You might even have a Roomba, a vacuuming robot, at home. Other robots are extraordinary. Some robots that look like people can walk and jump!

Robots do many jobs. They can even clean your house by vacuuming it, or sucking up all the dirt!

THINK ON YOUR OWN

What robots have you seen?

Helping Humans

Humans have been using machines for a long time. One simple machine is a pulley. A pulley is a wheel that a rope goes around. It makes lifting heavy items easier for people. Pulleys let people build huge buildings thousands of years ago. Some people think this is how the ancient pyramids of Egypt were built.

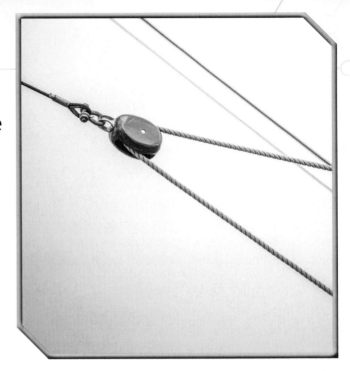

A pulley such as this one makes it easier to lift things that are heavy.

Pulleys and other simple machines aren't robots, though. Simple machines can't do work on their own. They need people to help them. Today, people are using robots more often. The power of computers makes it possible for robots to do more with less help from people.

Why Do We Have Robots?

Robots are built to do jobs so humans don't need to do them. Sometimes, it's faster or cheaper for robots to do something. For example, many factories use robots. A robotic arm is a common robot in factories. These arms do simple tasks over and over again. They're often faster than a person is. Sometimes, they're stronger too.

Some robots do jobs that aren't safe for people. Rovers are wheeled robots that explore the moon and Mars. No person has ever set foot on Mars. It would be a very long and dangerous, or unsafe, trip. However, a

Robotic arms are made to do jobs in all kinds of factories.

rover explored Mars for 15 years! On Earth, robots clean up dangerous things that humans don't want to get close to.

Rovers explore Mars and send *information* and photographs to scientists on Earth.

Some robots do jobs more easily than a human could. **Drones** fly over buildings and bridges to take pictures of them. These pictures help workers keep the buildings and bridges safe and clean. In the past, people could take these pictures from airplanes. However, flying an airplane is a lot harder than sending a drone to do this job.

THINK ON YOUR OWN

Why can robots do dangerous tasks that humans can't?

HOW ROBOTS WORK

2

Robots come in all different shapes and sizes. They're built for the job they need to do. Drones have rotors—blades that help them move through the air. Underwater robots have different blades that help them move through water. Some robots, such as robotic arms, move in place.

What Are Robots Made Of?

All robots have some things in common, even robots **designed** to do very different jobs. Robots need three special parts: a body, one or more sensors, and a control system.

◄ ··············

These robotic arms assemble, or put together, cars.

The body is the part of the robot that moves. The body of a robot is designed for the task it does. If the robot cleans, its body might have a vacuum cleaner. If it moves on the ground, it might have wheels or legs. Generally, robots have a motor. The motor powers their movement.

The body also houses the sensors and control system. Sensors gather information for the robot. They act like its eyes and ears. Sensors also help robots move. They sense things in the way so the robot can go around them.

The robot's control system, or brain, is what makes a robot a robot. Without it, the robot would just be a machine. The control system allows the robot to make decisions. For example, if a robotic arm in a

The motor in this robotic car turns its wheels and makes it go.

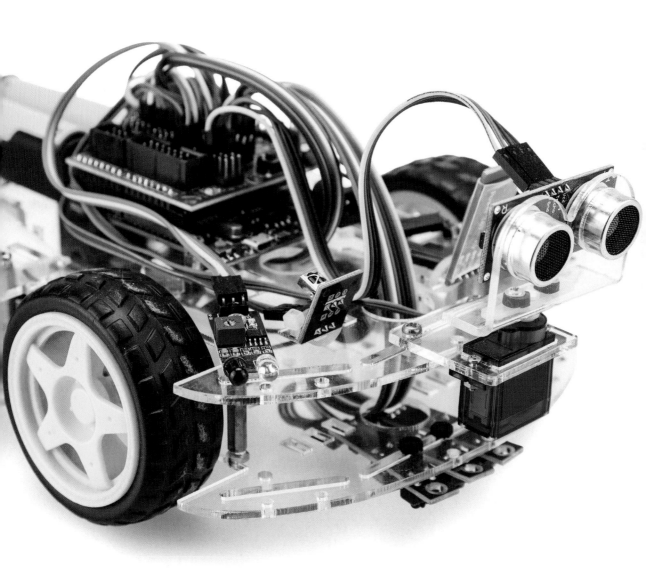

THINK ON YOUR OWN

What sensors do you think a robotic vacuum needs?

car factory senses there's no car part in front of it, it will stop working. The control system is what makes this decision.

Humans **program** the control system at first. However, once the robot starts working, it doesn't need help from humans anymore. Its "brain" tells it what to do.

Materials

Robots are built from many **materials**. Often, they have a metal frame. This makes them strong, so they won't break easily.

Plastic is another common material.

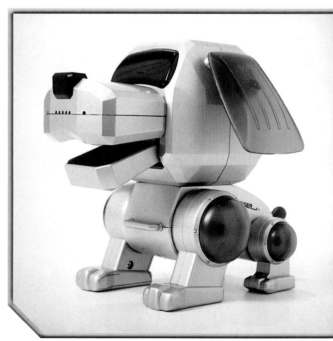

Some people have pet robots!

14

This robot is designed to gather litter from the water.

Plastic can be molded into many shapes. It's also lighter than metal. The outer body of many robots is made of plastic.

The control system of the robot is made of **circuits**. The circuits are like those in a computer. They hold the programs that tell the robot what to do.

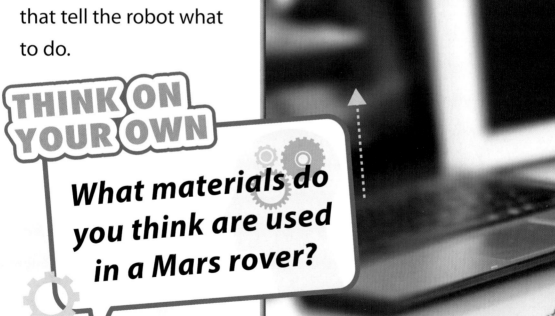

THINK ON YOUR OWN

What materials do you think are used in a Mars rover?

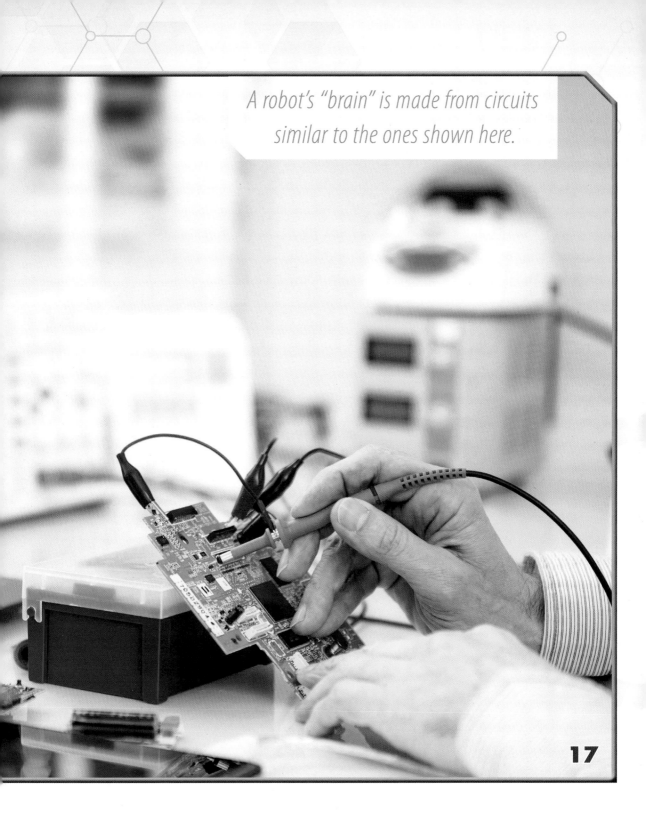

A robot's "brain" is made from circuits similar to the ones shown here.

3

BUILDING ROBOTS

Building a robot takes a lot of work. It also takes a lot of knowledge. Science, technology, **engineering**, and math (STEM) are all needed. Large teams of people often help design and build robots, including drones.

Designing Drones

Drones are some of the most popular robots today. They're used by the military, people at work, and people who just want to have fun. You can see them in parks around the world where people fly them as a hobby.

◀

Many people work together to build robots.

Making the kinds of drones used around the world today is a big job. Many engineers and computer programmers work long hours to design and build drones. They had to solve, or fix, countless problems, even after they made the first drone that could fly.

Armies around the world use drones to take photographs.

Drones are most often used for taking pictures and video. For example, at construction sites, drones take pictures of the land. This helps workers figure out where to build.

Drone Photography

It wasn't easy to make drones that could take pictures. Most drones are quadcopters. This means they have four rotors. The rotors spin, and the drone flies. This is amazing technology, but it meant the first drones shook slightly in the air. Pictures taken from the first drones were blurry, or unclear, because of the shaking.

Engineers needed a **solution** to this problem. They looked to a piece of old technology for an answer: the gimbal. A gimbal is a device that holds something steady. Gimbals were first used on ships. They kept ships steady when waves hit.

Drone engineers made new, smaller gimbals to hold cameras on drones. They made it so the camera didn't shake even

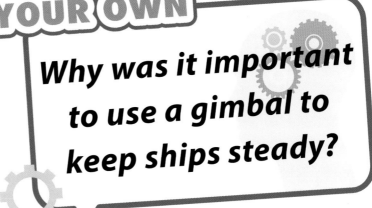

THINK ON YOUR OWN

Why was it important to use a gimbal to keep ships steady?

Cameras are often mounted on the bottom of drones. A gimbal holds them still.

though the drone holding it did. This is why drones can take clear photographs today.

Autopilot

Another problem that drones had was that it was hard for people to fly them and take pictures at the same time. While drones are designed to be easy to fly, it still takes some effort. Flying them is distracting when you're also trying to photograph something important.

To solve this problem, computer programmers designed autopilot for drones. Autopilot allows people to program drones and tell them where to go. The drone then flies along a route, or path, without any help from a human. This lets someone concentrate on just taking the right pictures or video.

Drones of all sizes can fly without people controlling them.

THINK ON YOUR OWN

Why are drones robots and not just machines?

23

ROBOTS IN THE FUTURE

4

Robots are becoming more and more advanced. In the future, they will do many tasks that humans still do today. Hopefully, this will make life easier and safer for people around the world.

Driverless Cars

One new technology people are excited about is driverless cars. Engineers are designing cars that will drive themselves. These are sometimes called autonomous cars. Autonomous means free from control. It's a word that's often used for robots since they act without help from humans.

Sometimes drivers don't see people, but driverless cars use sensors, not eyes, to "see" what's around them.

25

In the future, people will get into an autonomous car and tell it where they want to go. The car will take them there without the person having to drive at all. People believe this will make roads much safer than they are now. Many car accidents happen when people make mistakes. If every car on the road could **communicate** with other cars, mistakes wouldn't be as likely.

Some autonomous cars are already on the road, but it will be a long time before most people can buy one.

Today, there are still some problems with driverless cars. They have trouble guessing what humans will do.

When humans drive other cars poorly or walk into the street, autonomous cars can make mistakes. However, engineers are working to solve these problems.

Artificial Intelligence

Right now, robots can make decisions. For example, drones can sense objects they are flying toward. Even if their user is telling them to fly into it, they can decide to stop. This decision is programmed into the drone by the people who made it.

THINK ON YOUR OWN

What is one reason driverless cars can be safer than other cars?

In the future, robots may be able to teach themselves things. They won't need to have their decisions programmed by people. They will teach themselves how to do their task well through artificial intelligence (AI).

AI is a kind of "thinking" that machines do. Some machines can learn or solve problems. However, their ability to do this kind of thinking is still very limited. Computer programmers are trying to make AI better. One day, it may be possible for machines to teach themselves new skills and abilities.

These robots use their artificial intelligence to teach children.

THINK ON YOUR OWN

Can you think of a downside of artificial intelligence?

If AI gets better, it will mean robots will be able to really learn and solve problems. They won't need to use programs written by humans to decide what to do. It would be a major step forward.

Driverless cars and artificial intelligence are just two of the new kinds of technology being planned for robots. It's likely that robots will change how we do everyday tasks. Some businesses are already using robots to greet people! This might be common in the future, or it might be a fad. What's certain is robots are here to stay!

Robots may take the place of workers in restaurants and hotels one day.

Glossary

circuit A closed path made of wires or other parts that allows energy or electricity to pass through it.

communicate To share ideas and knowledge.

design A plan for something. Also, to create a plan for something.

drone A flying vehicle that can move without a pilot in it.

engineering The study and practice of using math and science to do useful things, such as building machines.

information Knowledge or facts about something.

material Something from which something else can be made.

program Instructions for a computer to follow. Also, the process of writing instructions for a computer to follow.

solution A way to fix a problem.

Find Out More

Books

Cassriel, Betsy. *Robot Builders!* Broomall, PA: Mason Crest, 2016.

DK. *Robot*. New York, NY: DK, 2018.

Stewart, Melissa. *Robots*. Washington, DC: National Geographic Kids, 2014.

Websites

Challenge: Robots!

nationalgeographic.org/interactive/challenge-robots
This fun game lets you build robots to solve problems.

Robots for Kids

sciencekids.co.nz/robots.html
This website features games and quizzes about robots of all kinds.

Index